K.E.Y.S To

'People First'

Leadership

Patsy Alston

© 2024 Patsy Alston. All rights reserved.

Table of Contents

Page	Content
5	Introduction
14	Chapter 1: K
29	Chapter 2: E
46	Chapter 3: Y
68	Chapter 4: S
87	Conclusion

"Why fit in when you were born to stand out?" — *Dr. Seuss*

Introduction:

Unlocking Leadership with the K.E.Y.S. Framework

Let's start with a question:

What does it take to be a truly great leader?

Leadership is one of those concepts that everyone talks about. What does it take to be a great leader? Ask 10 different people you'll probably get 10 different answers. Some will tell you it's about vision or execution. Others might talk about charisma or decision-making. And while all of these traits play a role, the truth is that leadership is much more complex than any single quality.

Leadership isn't about one big thing. It's about **how** you connect the dots between who you are, how you serve others, the results you achieve, and how you build something that lasts. True leadership is about connecting with others, guiding them, and creating lasting impact.

That's where the **K.E.Y.S. framework** comes in.

The K.E.Y.S. framework isn't just another set of abstract ideas—it was created to help leaders like you cut through the noise and focus on what really matters. It's a practical guide designed to help you become a leader who inspires trust, fosters innovation, drives results, and builds a legacy. Let's break down what this means and how you can use these principles to transform your leadership approach.

If you are a leader, the K.E.Y.S. framework will help you unlock your full leadership potential.

Why K.E.Y.S.?

Inside this book you will gain access to tools that will help you:

- **K – Know Yourself**: Self-awareness is the cornerstone of effective leadership. Knowing yourself means understanding your strengths, weaknesses, values, and how your actions affect others. Leaders who know themselves lead with authenticity and confidence. They're better equipped to handle challenges and connect meaningfully with their teams.

- **E – Empower Others**: Leadership is not a solo act. Empowering others means fostering an environment where your team feels trusted, valued, and capable of stepping into their potential. Empowered team members contribute more effectively and drive innovation, which benefits the whole organization. Your role is to inspire and create pathways for others to thrive.
- **Y – Yield Space and Results**: Leadership is about achieving outcomes, but it's also about the way you achieve them. Yielding results isn't just about pushing for metrics—it's about creating a balanced space where team members feel encouraged to contribute their ideas and solutions. When you yield space for your team's input, you foster a culture of trust and collaboration that leads to sustainable success.
- **S – Sustain Growth through Service**: The final key focuses on long-term impact. Sustaining growth isn't just about reaching new heights—it's about ensuring that progress can continue over time. This requires service-oriented

leadership—leading by example and putting the needs of the team first. By serving your team, fostering resilience, and supporting continuous learning, you create a foundation that sustains growth and nurtures future leaders.

The **K.E.Y.S. framework** isn't just a theory. It's a practical, action-oriented approach to leadership that helps you lead with clarity, purpose, and impact. These four keys work together to create a leadership style that's both effective and people-focused. And when you master them, you unlock not only your potential but the potential of everyone around you.

What This Book Will Help You Do

This book is designed to take you step-by-step through each part of the K.E.Y.S. framework. You'll get practical advice, real-life stories, and actionable strategies that you can apply immediately in your leadership journey. This isn't just a book to read—it's a guide to **leadership transformation**.

Why This Matters Now More Than Ever

We're living in a time where leadership is more challenging—and more important—than ever. With rapidly changing markets, evolving technology, and a workforce that's looking for meaning and purpose, leaders are being called to step up in new ways. That means the landscape of leadership is changing. In a world that demands adaptability, empathy, and a strong sense of purpose, leaders can no longer rely solely on traditional top-down methods. The most successful leaders are those who can balance results with relationships, push for progress while empowering others, and maintain growth by putting their team's needs first.

It's not enough to simply manage people or hit numbers. To be a great leader today, you need to connect with people on a deeper level, inspire them with a sense of purpose, and build an environment where they can thrive. The days of "command and control" leadership are long gone. Today's leaders need to be coaches, mentors, and visionaries.

The K.E.Y.S. framework is the mechanism to do just that. It's about leading in a way that's both people-focused and results-driven, enabling you to build a culture where everyone thrives and success is sustained. You'll have the tools to lead with confidence, empathy, and effectiveness. And more importantly, you'll be able to create lasting, meaningful impact—not just for your team or organization, but for yourself as well.

What to Expect

This isn't just another leadership book full of buzzwords and abstract concepts. This is a **practical guide** designed to help you take action. I've intentionally written this in a conversational style because I want you to feel like we're having a one-on-one conversation as you work through these ideas.

Each chapter of this book will guide you through one of the four keys. You'll find:

- **Real-world stories** that illustrate how these principles work in practice.

- **Actionable tips** to apply what you learn immediately.
- **Reflective questions** to help you assess your current leadership approach and identify areas for growth.
- You'll also find **questions and exercises** to help you apply the K.E.Y.S. framework in your own leadership.

The goal is to make these principles not just something you read but something you live and integrate into your daily leadership practice.

Your Leadership Journey Starts Now

The K.E.Y.S. framework is your roadmap to unlocking your full leadership potential. No matter the size of the team you are leading, these principles will help you create a positive, impactful, and lasting legacy.

You already have what it takes to be a great leader—it's within you. The K.E.Y.S. framework is here to help you unlock that potential. Whether you're a seasoned leader looking to sharpen your skills or someone stepping into leadership for the first time, this framework will refine your power to lead with credibility, impact, and purpose.

So grab a pen, get ready to reflect, and prepare to take action. Because leadership isn't something you master overnight—it's a journey. And every step you take toward knowing yourself, empowering others, yielding results, and sustaining growth will move you closer to becoming the leader you're meant to be.

"Today you are You, that is truer than true. There is no one alive who is Youer than You."
— Dr. Seuss

K

Chapter 1: Know Yourself

A Tale of Three Directors

Imagine walking into a room filled with your team—the people who rely on you for guidance, support, and direction and whom you rely on for results, productivity, and efficiency. In your imagination, picture that room weighed down by blame, frustration, and low morale. Now picture the room buzzing with energy, collaboration, and creativity.

What's the difference?

Leadership.

And not just any leadership, but **'People First' Leadership**—a style grounded in valuing people, believing in their potential, and ensuring they feel important. This kind of leadership transforms teams and organizations.

How do I know this? I learned through my own experiences in the executive world, under three very different directors. This real life case study is unique in that the three directors lead the same team, with the same middle management, the same directives and goals, but with very different outcomes. Each one taught me valuable lessons about leadership and how your focus shapes the outcomes of a team. Let's take a look at each example.

Leader #1: The Capable Manager

Managers manage and dictate.

They control situations, they put out fires, and often, they run the show.

Leaders empower and influence.

They guide, inspire, and then step back to let the team shine.

When I first joined the executive team, I was full of excitement and optimism. The director I worked under wasn't a bad person—she was personable, well spoken, and organized. But here's the catch: she wasn't a leader.

She was a manager stuck in a loop of blame and willful ignorance to her own weaknesses.

She was a brilliant 'doer' and a **capable manager**, but she lacked the self-awareness to recognize how her approach to the team stifled the department's growth. She implemented processes that were "good enough," but they failed to keep pace with the demands of our department and even though she had a brilliant team, she dismissed ideas from those working out those processes daily.

In the story of #1's career, she became the victim.

Even though the processes were hers, she would not own the outcomes. She blamed the workers for missed metrics. She started creating narratives in her mind of laziness, ignorance, and rebellion.

The more she blamed the team the harder it became to win her approval. It eventually trickled down into the team culture where blame shifting, frustration, and a 'us against them' mentality became the norm. Eroding the very thing she was trying to build.

Eventually, she was let go.

Leader #2: The Empowering Leader

After Leader #1 left, Leader #2 took over. She came in with a completely different mindset, and in just six months, our department transformed from struggling to excelling. What changed? The people? No. The circumstances? Nope. The leadership? Absolutely.

Leader #2 believed in people. She knew that the staff were capable, competent, and motivated. She empowered them to make decisions, solve problems, and contribute ideas. I felt the effect personally. I was the most junior member of the executive team, but she placed a weight on my ideas and thoughts like I was a senior leader, and under her guidance I thrived.

What set her apart? She knew her strengths and her weaknesses, and she wasn't afraid to ask for help. She communicated clearly and without blame. When something didn't work, instead of pointing fingers, she invited us to discuss what went wrong and how we could improve. Her leadership built trust and ownership, and as a result, we didn't just meet our goals—we surpassed them.

Leader #2 understood that leadership was about putting **people first**. She worked to remove obstacles, build trust, and create a culture of empowerment. She believed that when the team thrives, the results will follow.

Leader #3: The Disconnected Leader -

Eventually, Leader #2 was promoted to another organization, and Leader #3 stepped in. Initially, everything seemed fine.

Leader #3 understood that she needed to learn a new way of leadership interaction and agreed to mentorship. She really did want to continue the progress and thought with a few weeks of learning a new style, she would be as successful as her predecessor.

Unfortunately, she did not continue.

Leader #3 did not understand that it isn't just a 'leadership style', it's a redefinition of priorities, a realigning of thought processes, and a reimagining of relationship dynamics. So Leader #3 started strong but soon fell into the same trap as Leader #1.

The conversations in the executive office shifted from problem-solving to blame-shifting. When problems arose, they weren't addressed head-on; instead, they were brushed aside or blamed on external factors. She started thinking only about metrics, her reputation, and the reputation of the department and forgot to connect with those who made the reputation possible.

Over time, morale dropped, trust weakened, and the sense of teamwork cultivated by Leader #2 began to fade.

Leader #3 became so focused on the 'what' she became disconnected from the 'who.' She could clearly see the erosion in morale and the decline in metrics, but couldn't recognize that her viewpoints were contributing to the breakdown of the team's culture.

By the time I left, the team was struggling, and the positive energy that once filled the room was gone.

Why Knowing Yourself is the Foundation of Leadership

So, what's the takeaway from these stories? Leadership isn't about how much control you have, how skilled you are, or how many processes you can implement. It's about **knowing yourself**. Self-awareness is the foundation upon which great leadership is built. Without it, even the most well-intentioned leaders can fall into patterns that undermine their effectiveness.

When you know yourself—your strengths, weaknesses, motivations, and blind spots—you can lead with clarity and authenticity. Self-awareness allows you to align your leadership style with your values and adapt to the needs of your team. It fosters emotional intelligence, helping you build stronger connections with those you lead.

Self-awareness sets exceptional leaders apart from average ones. It helps you stay grounded and intentional. Leaders who know themselves can communicate transparently, make thoughtful decisions, and respond to challenges with confidence. But self-awareness isn't just about knowing your strengths—it's about understanding your weaknesses too.

When you embrace your strengths, you can lead from a place of authenticity and confidence. When you acknowledge your weaknesses, you can empower those around you to fill in the gaps.

The most successful leaders aren't the ones who know everything—they're the ones who know when to ask for help.

Self-Assessment Tools for Personal Leadership Discovery

Becoming more self-aware doesn't happen overnight. It requires reflection, feedback, and intentional growth. Here are some tools to help you on this journey:

- **Personality Assessments** (e.g., Myers-Briggs, Big Five): These tests offer insights into how you perceive the world, make decisions, and interact with others. Understanding your personality type can help you communicate more effectively and navigate team dynamics.

- **Emotional Intelligence (EQ) Assessments**: EQ is all about understanding and managing your emotions and those of others. Leaders with high EQ are better at building relationships, handling stress, and resolving conflicts.
- **360-Degree Feedback**: This method allows you to gather input from colleagues, direct reports, and supervisors. It reveals how others perceive your strengths and weaknesses, giving you a fuller picture of your leadership impact.
- **Leadership Style Assessments**: Are you more transformational or transactional? Understanding your default leadership style helps you adapt to different situations and team needs.

These are not 'one and done' assessments. As you continually refine your self-awareness and leadership approach, you will need to keep track of your growth and evolvement by reevaluating frequently.

Developing Emotional Intelligence (EQ)

Emotional intelligence is a hallmark of effective leadership. High EQ allows you to connect with your team on a deeper level, build trust, and navigate the complexities of interpersonal relationships. Here's how you can develop the key components of EQ:

- **Self-Regulation**: This is about managing your emotions, staying calm under pressure, and avoiding impulsive decisions. As a leader, your team looks to you for stability. When you can regulate your emotions, you set a positive example for others.
- **Empathy**: Empathy is the ability to put yourself in someone else's shoes. It helps you understand your team's needs, build stronger relationships, and resolve conflicts. Empathetic leaders don't just see people as workers—they see them as individuals with unique needs and perspectives.
- **Self-Motivation**: Great leaders are driven by internal values and goals, not just external rewards. When you know what motivates you, you can stay focused on long-term success, even in the face of setbacks.

The Role of Mindset in Leadership

Your mindset plays a critical role in how you approach challenges, setbacks, and growth opportunities. Leaders with a **fixed mindset** believe their abilities are static—they avoid challenges, resist feedback, and fear failure. In contrast, leaders with a **growth mindset** believe they can improve through effort and learning. They see challenges as opportunities to grow, embrace feedback, and are resilient in the face of adversity.

Cultivating a growth mindset will help you continue evolving as a leader. It encourages you to seek out new learning experiences, push beyond your comfort zone, help you rely on others around you for the success of the team, and embrace failure as a stepping stone to success.

The Role of Mentoring in Self-Awareness

Self-awareness doesn't develop in isolation. Mentorship is one of the most powerful tools for accelerating personal growth as a leader. Whether you're being mentored by someone or mentoring others, the process of giving and receiving guidance deepens your understanding of yourself.

Mentorship is a continuous cycle. As you grow as a leader, you'll seek guidance from mentors and simultaneously pass your knowledge on to the next generation of leaders.

Practical Steps for Deepening Self-Awareness

Here are a few actionable strategies to help you on your journey toward greater self-awareness:

- **Daily Reflection**: Set aside 10 minutes at the end of each day to reflect on your leadership actions. Ask yourself: *What went well today? What could I have done differently?*
- **Seek Feedback**: Regularly ask for feedback from your peers, team members, and mentors. This external perspective will help you see blind spots and areas for growth.

- **Keep a Leadership Journal**: Document your thoughts, challenges, and insights in a leadership journal. Writing helps clarify your thinking and track your progress over time.
- **Develop a Personal Growth Plan**: Identify your top strengths and weaknesses, and create a plan to leverage your strengths and improve on your weaknesses.

Key Takeaways

- Leadership begins with **self-awareness**. The more you understand yourself—your strengths, weaknesses, and emotional patterns—the more effective you will be in leading others.
- **Emotional intelligence** is critical to navigating relationships and team dynamics. By improving your EQ, you enhance your ability to connect with others and manage challenges effectively.
- Cultivating a **growth mindset** will help you embrace challenges, learn from feedback, and continuously improve as a leader.

- **Mentorship** accelerates self-awareness by providing guidance, perspective, and support. Whether you are being mentored or mentoring others, the process fosters growth and development.

Conclusion

As you continue to reflect, grow, and learn from your experiences, your leadership will evolve. The more self-aware you become, the more authentic and impactful your leadership will be. With self-awareness as your foundation, you are well-equipped to empower others, drive results, and sustain long-term growth.

"Unless someone like you cares a whole awful lot, nothing is going to get better. It's not."

— Dr. Seuss, The Lorax

E

Chapter 2: Empower Others

Why Empowerment is at the Heart of Great Leadership

Let's be honest: as a leader, there's only so much you can do on your own. Your ability to create real, lasting impact comes not from what *you* can accomplish, but from what your **team** can accomplish. That's where empowerment comes in.

Empowering others is not just a leadership strategy—it's the cornerstone of people-first leadership. When you empower others, you're unlocking their potential, building their confidence, and creating an environment where everyone can contribute their best. In the long run, it's the difference between being a manager and being a transformational leader.

But here's the challenge: empowerment doesn't happen overnight. It's a process that requires trust, communication, patience, and sometimes even stepping back so others can step up. It's about giving your team the tools they need to thrive and then trusting them to use those tools.

What Does Empowerment Actually Mean?

Before we dive into the "how," let's define what we really mean by **empowerment**. You've probably heard the word thrown around in leadership books or seminars, but at its core, empowerment is about **giving people the authority, confidence, and resources to take ownership of their work**.

In the previous chapter I alluded to a point in the story where Leader #2 affected my growth and my place on the team. As the most junior member of the executive team I was used to being in the room but not actually a part of the 'bigger' conversation. My experience was in administrative logistics and staff retention, but Leader #1 was not actually interested in my take on those subjects, so I remained quiet.

Once Leader #2 came in and realized that my strengths went beyond where I was actually situated within the department, she *empowered* me to walk in those strengths, frequently asked for my opinions on policy on those topics and others. She even reorganized some of my tasks and took things off of my plate so that I could operate in those spaces. Her 'outside of the box' thinking was rewarded. As a result of the practices I helped create and implement, we decreased departmental spending and turnover. Although this made her look like a hero to upper management, she made sure that myself and others on my team were recognized for our groundbreaking initiatives.

When someone feels empowered, they don't just follow orders; they think critically, solve problems creatively, and take initiative. They don't wait for instructions—they see what needs to be done and step up to do it. Empowerment isn't about letting go of leadership, it's about **sharing** it, so that everyone feels they have a stake in the success of the team.

The Empowerment Shift: From Task-Oriented to People-Oriented Leadership

One of the biggest shifts a leader can make is moving from task-oriented leadership to people-oriented leadership.

Task-oriented leaders focus on the "what" that needs to be done, how fast it can be completed, and the specific steps to get there.

People-oriented leaders focus on the "who" doing the work, how they feel about it, and how you can support them in growing through the process.

Let me tell you, when you focus on people first, the tasks eventually take care of themselves. Empowering others isn't about delegating tasks—it's about developing people. It's about recognizing that your team members are your greatest asset and giving them the space, trust, and responsibility to rise to the occasion.

The Two Non-Renewable Resources: Time and People

Here's something I want you to consider: everything in your organization is renewable. You can always make more money, win more clients, create more products. But there are two things you can never replace: **time** and **people**.

You might be wondering:

"But aren't there more people born every day?

How can people be non-renewable?"

Well, here's the thing—there's only **one of each person**. Once I'm gone from this earth, there will never be another *me*. Just as there was only one King David, one Esther, and one Nelson Mandela. In the same way, there will never be another team like the one you have assembled right now. The chemistry, the skills, the individual contributions—they're irreplaceable.

As a leader, you have to choose how you'll invest these two non-renewable resources: **time** and **people**. It's a choice you'll make every single day. Do you focus on people and sacrifice time, or do you focus on time and sacrifice people? And what are the outcomes of each?

Let's explore.

Focusing on People: The Long Game of Empowerment

If you choose to focus on people first, here's what happens: you *will* sacrifice **time** on the front end. It might feel like things are moving slowly at first because your team needs time to grow. You're not just telling them what to do—you're teaching them how to think for themselves, how to solve problems, and how to take ownership of their work. This process takes patience. But here's the beautiful part: once your team members are empowered, they become more creative, more independent, and more effective. Over time, the curve starts to shift, and your initial time investment starts to pay off. Your empowered team is now able to work efficiently without constant oversight. The result? You gain back time while the team's productivity soars.

Think about it like this: by focusing on people first, you're creating **problem solvers** rather than a team full of problems. You're building leaders who take initiative, think critically, and handle challenges on their own.

Focusing on Time: The Short-Term Trap

Now let's look at the alternative: focusing on **time** first. If your priority is getting things done as quickly as possible, you may hit your short-term targets, but there's a hidden cost. When you focus solely on time, you tend to focus on **outcomes** rather than **people**. You end up pushing for results without giving your team the space to learn and grow.

And here's where it gets tricky. When you neglect people, you don't just lose those who contribute the least. You lose the team members who contribute the **most**—the ones with the creativity, problem-solving abilities, and leadership potential. Once they're gone, their unique skills, knowledge, and influence go with them. You can't replace them, and you're left scrambling to find someone who might come close, but it's never quite the same.

So what happens? Your productivity dips, the team's dynamics change, and you end up losing even more **time** trying to fix the damage. Focusing on time first creates a vicious cycle where you're constantly trying to regain what you've lost. The only thing you're gaining in this scenario is **chaos**.

Building a Culture of Empowerment

Okay, so now that we've seen the importance of focusing on people, how do we actually build a culture of empowerment? It's one thing to talk about it, but creating an empowered team requires consistent action and intentional leadership.

Here's a roadmap for building that culture:

1. **Trust Your People**: The foundation of empowerment is trust. So, trust the hiring process. Your team was created by carefully screening for the skills and personalities you needed, and they need to know that you believe in them. That doesn't mean you turn a blind eye

to mistakes, but it does mean giving them the freedom to try, fail, and learn. When your team feels trusted, they're more willing to take initiative and take ownership of their work.

2. **Delegate Authority, Not Just Tasks**: There's a huge difference between delegating tasks and delegating authority. Delegating tasks is about getting things off your plate. Delegating authority is about giving your team the power to make decisions. When you delegate authority, you're telling your team, "I trust your judgment. You've got this." That's empowering.

3. **Create a Safe Space for Failure**: Let's face it—people are going to make mistakes. They *are* going to try things that *will not* work. It's inevitable. The key is how you respond. If you create an environment where failure is seen as a learning opportunity rather than a disaster, you're giving your team the freedom to innovate. Mistakes become stepping stones rather than stumbling blocks.

4. **Celebrate Wins, Big and Small**: Empowerment thrives in a culture of recognition. When someone on your team steps up, takes ownership, or

solves a problem, **celebrate** it. Recognition doesn't have to be elaborate—it can be as simple as a shout-out in a team meeting or a quick "thank you" email. The point is to show your team that their contributions matter.

5. **Provide Resources and Support**: Empowerment isn't about throwing your team into the deep end and walking away. It's about giving them the tools, resources, and support they need to succeed. This might mean providing training, offering guidance, or removing obstacles that are getting in their way. Your role as a leader is to equip your team to do their best work.

The Role of Feedback in Empowerment

Empowerment isn't a one-way street. It requires ongoing communication, support, and—most importantly—**feedback**. Without feedback, your team won't know what's working, what isn't, and how they can improve. But not all feedback is created equal.

Here's how you can give feedback that truly empowers:

- **Make It Constructive**: Feedback should be specific, actionable, and focused on growth. Instead of saying, "This didn't work," try, "How can we improve this next time?" The goal is to guide your team toward solutions, not just point out problems.
- **Be Balanced**: Don't wait until something goes wrong to give feedback. If you only point out mistakes, your team will start to feel discouraged. Make a habit of giving **positive feedback** too. Recognize the things your team is doing well and encourage them to build on those strengths.
- **Encourage Self-Reflection**: Sometimes the best feedback comes from within. Encourage your team to reflect on their own performance. Ask questions like, "What do you think went well?" or "How do you think we can improve this process?" By fostering self-reflection, you're helping your team develop their own sense of accountability, and possibly discovering solutions that are only seen from their vantage point.

The Ripple Effect of Empowerment

Here's the best part about empowering others: when you do it right, the impact goes far beyond the individual. Empowerment creates a **ripple effect**. As one person steps into their potential, they inspire others to do the same. The team becomes more cohesive, more collaborative, and more innovative. And as the team rises, so do the results.

Empowerment isn't just about making your life easier as a leader, because often you will have to be more intentional and observant, it's about creating a team culture where everyone thrives. The more empowered your team feels, the more they contribute to the success of the organization. It's a win-win.

Empowering in Action: A Case Study

Let me share a quick story from my own experience. In the aftermath of Hurricane Katrina, the scale of devastation was unimaginable, and the need for volunteers; immense. As the Volunteer Disaster

Coordinator for the American Red Cross in that area, my focus shifted from immediate relief to preparing for the future. Local volunteers, exhausted and overwhelmed, were already stretched to their limits. The answer was surprising.

When volunteers started arriving from various organizations across the country and the world to help out with the clean up and rebuild of the damaged areas. Though many had different experiences and levels of expertise, they all shared a common passion: the drive to help. These volunteers, however, had their own needs. For example, many would require shelter and support in the event of future disasters. And in a time where the resources and infrastructure was already thin, that could have been another issue to deal with.

But rather than see this as a limitation, I saw an opportunity. I realized that within their need, there was room for empowerment. By addressing their vulnerability head-on, I could help transform it into a source of strength.

Our team developed a system that not only answered their possible need for shelter, but also tapped into their desire to serve by training them as shelter workers. Through partnerships with these other organizations, we created a program that equipped the volunteers with the skills to manage shelters and prepared them for the possibility of a future crisis. It was more than just training—it was empowering them to take ownership of the relief effort, even in the face of their own challenges.

What emerged was a resilient network of volunteers who could serve and lead, even as they faced personal hardships. The program turned what could have been a point of weakness and strain of already stretched resources into a powerful asset. These volunteers became more than helpers—they became empowered leaders, ready to meet the challenges ahead.

This experience taught me a profound truth: even in people's moments of need and weakness there are always opportunities to empower them. By addressing both their vulnerabilities and their passions, you can unlock potential that not only meets the immediate need but also prepares them to lead with confidence in the future.

Key Takeaways

- Empowering others is about giving people the **authority, confidence, and resources** to take ownership of their work.
- Focusing on people first requires an investment of **time**, but in the long run, it pays off in increased productivity, creativity, and independence.
- Feedback is a critical part of empowerment—make it constructive, balanced, focused on growth, and collaborative.
- Building a culture of empowerment creates a **ripple effect** where individuals and teams rise together.

Conclusion

Empowerment is more than a leadership buzzword—it's the foundation of transformational leadership. When you empower others, you're building more than just a team; you're building a culture of trust, ownership, and innovation. By focusing on people, creating a safe space for growth, and giving constructive feedback, you unlock the full potential of your team. And in doing so, you set the stage for long-term success—for them, and for you.

"Step with care and great tact, and remember that life's a great balancing act." — Dr. Seuss, Oh, the Places You'll Go!

Y

Chapter 3: Yield: Creating Space for Results and Contributions

Why Results Matter and How to Achieve Them Without Losing Your People Along the Way

Let's talk results. As a leader, there's no escaping the fact that you're judged by what you deliver. Whether you're leading a business, a department, or even a family, people look to you to get things done. And, yes, results matter. But **how** you achieve those results is just as important—if not more so—than the results themselves.

Now let's talk about the word 'yield' When you hear that word what comes to mind?

Is it production, results, or harvest?

Maybe slowing down, giving way, or making room?

In leadership, it's not just about producing results; it's about creating space for others to step forward, share their insights, and take ownership. Great leaders understand that success is never a solo act—it's a symphony of contributions, where everyone has a role.

The truth is, if you focus solely on outcomes—pushing for metrics and KPIs (Key Performance Indicators) while neglecting the well-being of your team—you might get short-term wins, but you'll also burn people out, lose your best talent, and ultimately sabotage your long-term success.

The question is then, are you in it for the short game or a long game?

If you're looking for a long game with increasing results over a period of time, yielding as a leader means fostering an environment where your team feels empowered to contribute their ideas, skills, and energy. It's about collaboration, trust, and nurturing a collective effort that drives results and fuels innovation. When leaders yield space for their teams, they achieve not just better outcomes, but a culture rooted in trust and creativity.

So, how do you **yield results** without sacrificing your people in the process? That's what we're going to dive into here.

The Danger of Results Without Purpose

As we've discussed in previous chapters, this is the main thing that turns leaders into managers: they become obsessed with outcomes but lose sight of the people producing those outcomes. We've all seen it—the pressure to hit numbers, meet quotas, and deliver results can sometimes cause leaders to treat their teams like machines instead of humans. And let me tell you, that approach backfires every time.

When you push people to achieve results without helping them understand the purpose, you might get compliance, but you'll never get commitment. And compliance alone is a short road to burnout and turnover.

So yes, you might hit the goal, but at what cost? The truth is, **sacrificing people for results** is a losing game.

Putting Yielding into Practice

To yield effectively, you need to be intentional about listening and creating spaces. Here's how you can put this into practice:

1. **Facilitate Open Discussions:** Create an environment where your team feels comfortable sharing ideas without judgment. Simple questions like, "What do you think?" or "How would you approach this?" can open the door to valuable input.
2. **Delegate with Trust:** Don't just assign tasks—delegate responsibilities. Let your team own projects from start to finish, trusting that every decision will either lead to a success or that they will learn from their experiences.
3. **Model Active Listening:** Show genuine interest in what your team has to say. Practice active listening by acknowledging contributions, asking follow-up questions, and building on their ideas.
4. **Create Safe Spaces for Failure:** Growth and innovation come with the risk of failure. Leaders who yield space must create an environment

where failure is seen as a step toward learning, not a reason for blame.

The 'Why' Behind the 'What': Finding Purpose in Metrics

Focusing on the outcomes—metrics, targets, and bottom line—is natural. But here's the thing: the path you take to achieve those results is just as important as the results themselves. A leader that is so focused on hitting short-term goals, piles on the pressure, micromanages the process, and burns out their best employees. They forget that their job is leading people, not just managing numbers. They may get a win this quarter, but they end up losing key people in the long run—people who were integral to the team's success. And guess what? Once those people are gone, so is the knowledge, creativity, and influence they brought to the table.

Let's start with a story that shaped my perspective on results and metrics.

Let me take you back to a time when I was part of an executive team leading a fast-paced, high-pressure department. We worked in an environment where everything was measured. Time was tracked down to the second. Productivity metrics were scrutinized, and client satisfaction was logged meticulously. We had dashboards, reports, and numbers for just about every aspect of our operations, and those metrics were available for anyone to see—daily.

Now, most organizations would have used these numbers to drive their teams harder, constantly reminding them to hit targets and improve results. It's easy to fall into the trap of becoming a "metrics machine," where everything revolves around the numbers and how well people are performing against them. But we decided to take a different path. We wanted to make sure that the metrics weren't just a stick to beat people, but a tool for fostering real growth and engagement.

Here's how we made that happen.

Instead of slapping the numbers on the table and saying, "Here's where you fell short," we began every review with questions like, "What went right?" and "How can we build on this?" It wasn't just about celebrating wins; it was about uncovering the behaviors, decisions, and processes that led to success. We wanted to replicate those successes, not just once, but consistently. That meant digging into the details with a positive future-focused perspective.

When the numbers weren't so great, we didn't fall into the trap of blame. Instead, we used the metrics as a starting point for constructive dialogue. We asked, "What's holding us back from reaching these goals?" and "How can we change that?" These conversations weren't punitive; they were collaborative. Our focus was on understanding the barriers and finding solutions together. The numbers didn't control us—they helped us grow.

This process of engaging the team in the 'why' behind the 'what' completely changed the atmosphere. No longer were the metrics something to fear; they became a tool for empowerment. Team members started owning their results. They saw metrics not as abstract data points but as indicators of how their contributions aligned with the larger mission of the department. And when people understand the why behind what they're doing, it unleashes a deeper level of engagement.

For example, we had a team struggling with time management. Rather than chastise them for missing targets, we examined what was happening on the ground. We found that part of the issue wasn't skill or effort—it was a lack of communication across departments. Once we pinpointed that, we worked together to set up systems that improved cross-functional collaboration. Almost immediately, their productivity increased and they consistently hit their targets after that.

Another team was having difficulty maintaining client satisfaction. Again, instead of focusing solely on the numbers, we dug into the reasons. It became clear that clients needed more frequent updates, even if there were only minor changes since the previous communication. Armed with this insight, we designated a certain department to update and define outcomes, ensuring expectations were clearer during the whole of the client journey. Satisfaction scores soared.

The lesson I learned during that time was simple yet profound: metrics, data, and results are essential, but they're just tools. If you only focus on the numbers, you're missing the point. The real magic happens when you align those numbers with a clear purpose—when your team understands not just what they're doing but why it matters. When they grasp the significance of their work, they become more than employees—they become empowered contributors to the mission.

In the end, we didn't just meet our metrics—we exceeded them, year after year. Not because we pushed harder, but because we focused on the bigger picture. We used the metrics to foster growth, not to control. We aligned our purpose with the indicators of performance, and the results were extraordinary.

That's the true power of understanding the 'why' behind the 'what.' It transforms a team from simply hitting targets to truly owning the process, unlocking their potential, and driving success in ways that go far beyond the numbers.

Creating a Results-Driven Culture Without the Burnout

So, how do you create a culture that drives results but also nurtures and sustains your team? As we just discussed, it starts with balancing the **'what'** and the **'why'**—being clear about the outcomes you need while ensuring your team is supported, valued, and aligned with the bigger purpose.

Here's how to do it:

1. **Set Clear, Measurable Goals**: Your team can't hit a target they can't see. Start by clearly defining what success looks like. This isn't just about high-level goals but about breaking them down into measurable steps. Make sure each person on your team knows their role in achieving these goals, and more importantly, why their contribution matters.

2. **Connect the Dots Between Effort and Impact**: It's easy for team members to get lost in the day-to-day grind, checking off tasks without understanding how those tasks connect to the bigger picture. As a leader, it's your job to help them see the connection. Let them know how their work impacts the team, the organization, and even the clients or customers they serve.

When people understand the **why**, they're more motivated and invested.

3. **Celebrate the Wins—Big and Small**: One thing I learned early in my leadership journey is the importance of celebrating progress. Results-driven cultures aren't just about hitting big milestones—they're about recognizing the small wins along the way. When you acknowledge the effort and progress your team is making, you build momentum. It doesn't have to be a big celebration—sometimes a simple "thank you" or acknowledgment in a team meeting can make all the difference.

4. **Focus on Growth Conversations, Not Just Performance Reviews**: Performance reviews can be helpful to see where you are coming from, but cannot tell you where you are going. Real growth happens when you have **forward-looking conversations**. Ask questions like, "How can we continue this success?" and "What do you need to keep growing?" When your team feels like their development is a priority, they're more likely to be invested in delivering results.

The Importance of Accountability (And How to Do It Right)

Let's talk about accountability. Holding your team accountable is critical to achieving results, but it's also one of the trickiest parts of leadership. Done poorly, accountability can feel like micromanaging or finger-pointing. Done well, it creates a sense of ownership and responsibility.

So how do you hold people accountable without demotivating them? Here's the key: **accountability should always come with support.** If someone isn't hitting their targets, don't just say, "You need to do better." Ask, *"What's getting in the way of your success, and how can I help remove those barriers?"*

- **Shift from Blame to Problem-Solving**: Instead of focusing on what's gone wrong, focus on how you can fix it together. Approach accountability from a place of support, not blame. This builds trust and encourages people to speak up when they're struggling, rather than hiding mistakes or setbacks.

- **Set Expectations Upfront**: Accountability works best when expectations are clear from the start. Make sure your team knows what's expected of them and what success looks like. That way, there are no surprises when it's time to review progress.
- **Follow Through on Feedback**: If you're going to hold someone accountable, you also need to provide feedback—and not just when something goes wrong. Positive reinforcement goes a long way in encouraging the behaviors and actions that lead to results. When someone hits their goals or makes progress, let them know you see it. That recognition fuels future success.

Adaptability: The Secret to Sustained Results

Here's something I've learned over the years: **things change**. The market shifts, new challenges emerge, and sometimes, the strategies that worked yesterday don't work today. That's why one of the most important traits in leadership—and in delivering results—is adaptability.

You can set all the goals in the world, but if you're not willing to pivot when circumstances change, you'll struggle to sustain success. The best leaders are those who are willing to adapt, to ask new questions, and to try new approaches when necessary.

Here's how to foster adaptability in your results-driven culture:

- **Encourage Experimentation**: Let your team know that it's okay to try new things, even if they don't always work out. Create a culture where experimentation is encouraged, and where failures are seen as opportunities to learn, not reasons to punish.
- **Be Willing to Pivot**: If something isn't working, don't be afraid to change course. Holding on to a strategy just because it worked in the past can hold you back. Regularly assess your progress and be open to adjusting your approach.
- **Stay Focused on the Long Game**: While short-term wins are important, sustaining results

means keeping your eyes on the long-term vision. Don't get so caught up in today's numbers that you lose sight of where you want to go in the future. Adaptability is key to balancing both.

Case Study: Metrics with Meaning

Let's circle back to the story I shared earlier in this chapter. The executive team I was part of wasn't just successful because we had the right metrics in place—we were successful because we used those metrics as tools for growth, not as weapons for pressure.

We constantly asked questions like:

- "How can we continue this success?"
- "What barriers are getting in the way of our progress?"
- "How can we grow and improve?"

We turned the data into conversations. And these conversations weren't about blame or criticism—they were about finding solutions, identifying opportunities, and getting better as a team.

The key takeaway here is that metrics, by themselves, are neutral. They're just numbers. What gives them meaning is how you use them. If you use them to beat people down, they'll fear the numbers. But if you use them to inspire growth, they'll see the metrics as a tool for improvement.

When our team shifted to this growth-focused mindset, we didn't just hit our targets, we smashed them. People felt empowered to take ownership of the data, look for ways to improve, and bring their own creative solutions to the table. And because we aligned the **'what'** with the **'why'**, the results followed naturally.

How to Use Metrics as a Tool for Growth

Let's get into the nitty-gritty of how you can use metrics to drive results without losing your people in the process. Remember, metrics are just data—they're not the enemy. But how you frame those metrics and what you do with the information makes all the difference.

Here's how to use metrics as a **tool for growth**:

- **Start with the Big Picture**: Before diving into individual performance metrics, make sure your team understands the broader goals of the organization. What's the vision? What's the mission? How do these metrics contribute to that larger purpose? When people know how their work fits into the overall mission, they're more likely to stay motivated and invested in the outcome.
- **Turn Data into Dialogue**: Metrics should spark conversations, not dread. Use the data as a jumping-off point for meaningful discussions about what's working and what isn't. Ask your team for their input—what barriers are they facing? What do they need to succeed? By involving them in the process, you empower them to take ownership of the results.
- **Focus on the Growth, Not Just the Gap**: When you're reviewing metrics with your team, don't just focus on where they fell short. Celebrate where they've made progress and highlight what went right. Then, identify the areas where there's room for improvement and frame it as an opportunity for growth, not failure.

- **Create Actionable Next Steps**: Once you've reviewed the data and had the conversation, it's time to create actionable steps for moving forward. What can your team do differently? What resources do they need to improve? Make sure these steps are clear, specific, and attainable.

Empower Your Team to Own the Results

A huge part of yielding results comes down to **ownership**. When your team feels like they have a stake in the outcome, they're more likely to push harder, think creatively, and problem-solve on their own. But ownership doesn't happen automatically—it's something you, as the leader, have to nurture.

Here's how to empower your team to own the results:

- **Give Them Autonomy**: One of the quickest ways to kill ownership is by micromanaging. When you dictate every move, your team doesn't feel like they have any real control over the outcome. Instead, give them the freedom to make decisions. Let them take the lead on projects and come up with solutions on their own. When people feel like they're trusted, they step up.

- **Encourage Creativity**: Results-driven cultures thrive on creativity. Encourage your team to think outside the box. Let them know that it's okay to experiment and try new approaches. When people are given the space to innovate, they often come up with solutions that are even better than what you originally envisioned.
- **Create a Safe Space for Failure**: Let's be real—failure is part of the process. If your team is afraid of messing up, they'll play it safe, and safe doesn't drive results. Create an environment where failure is seen as a learning opportunity, not a disaster. When people know they won't be punished for trying something new, they're more likely to take risks—and those risks often lead to breakthroughs.

Key Takeaways

- Results matter, but **how** you achieve them matters more. Focus on both the outcomes and the people behind them.
- Metrics are tools for growth, not weapons of pressure. Use data to spark conversations, drive improvement, and celebrate wins.
- Empower your team to take ownership of the results by giving them autonomy, encouraging creativity, and creating a safe space for failure.

Conclusion

In leadership, results are the proof of your impact. But the path to those results makes all the difference. By aligning your team with a clear purpose, using metrics as tools for growth, and empowering them to take ownership of the outcomes, you create a culture where both people and results thrive. And when you play the long game—balancing short-term wins with sustainable success—you set yourself and your team up for lasting impact.

So, let's not just chase numbers. Let's pursue results with purpose, with people at the forefront, and with the confidence that when we lead with intention, the results will follow.

"Will you succeed? Yes, you will indeed! (98 and 3/4 percent guaranteed.)" — *Dr. Seuss, Oh, the Places You'll Go!*

S

Chapter 4: Sustain Growth Through Service and Leadership

Why Sustaining Growth Through Service and Leadership is Just as Important as Achieving It

Here's a hard truth: growth, by itself, isn't the goal. Sure, it's exciting to hit milestones, grow your team, or expand your business, but real success comes from your ability to **sustain** that growth over time. Growth that isn't maintained is just a temporary win, and temporary wins are exactly that—temporary. What you really want is growth that lasts.

Leaders who can maintain momentum without losing sight of their core values and people are the ones who build legacies. Sustaining growth is not just about expanding reach or revenue—it's about nurturing an environment where people thrive, ideas flourish, and progress becomes the standard. To do this effectively, leaders must embody **S – Service**: leading by example and putting the needs of the team first.

When leaders commit to serving their teams, they create a culture of mutual trust and respect that fuels long-term success. Service in leadership means stepping in to support, guide, and empower others so that growth is not just a flash in the pan but a continuous journey.

Sustaining growth means more than just keeping the momentum going. It means creating a foundation strong enough to support ongoing success without burning out yourself or your team. It's about building systems that scale, fostering a culture of continuous improvement, and preparing for future challenges so that your growth isn't just a spike—it's a steady climb.

Let's dig into how you can **sustain growth** in your leadership and organization, because the work doesn't stop once you've achieved that initial success. In fact, it's just beginning.

Sustain Growth: The Foundation

To sustain growth, you need more than just short-term strategies; you need a long-term mindset that balances people, processes, and progress. Sustaining growth means building systems that can handle scaling without compromising quality or team morale. It's about fostering an environment where everyone can contribute to collective goals and see the value of their work in a larger context. The world changes too fast for you to stay still. Markets shift, technologies advance, industries evolve—and if you're not growing, you're falling behind. The most successful leaders are the ones who understand that growth and learning go hand in hand.

Here's what it takes to sustain growth:
- **Invest in Continuous Learning:** A team that stops learning is a team that stops growing. Encourage ongoing education, skill development, and knowledge sharing. When leaders prioritize learning, they set an example for the entire team to follow.
    - **Commit to Personal Growth**: First and foremost, it starts with you. If you're not

growing as a leader, your team will stagnate too. Whether it's reading leadership books, attending workshops, or seeking out mentors, you should constantly be looking for ways to improve. The moment you think you've "arrived" is the moment you stop growing. Always be curious, always be open to learning.

- **Adapt and Innovate:** Sustaining growth requires flexibility. The strategies that worked yesterday may not work tomorrow. Be open to change and encourage your team to do the same. Innovation isn't just about big, groundbreaking ideas—it's about making small, continuous improvements that add up over time.
- **Empower Future Leaders:** Growth can only be sustained if there are others ready to step up and lead. Identify potential leaders within your team and invest in their development. When you build a pipeline of strong, capable leaders, you create a self-sustaining system where growth can continue even in your absence. Encourage your team to seek out opportunities for development, whether that's through training,

cross-departmental collaboration, or even taking on new challenges. When you create a culture where learning is valued and encouraged, growth becomes a natural outcome.

One of the most valuable things I've learned about leadership can be summed up with a quote attributed to John F. Kennedy, **"A rising tide lifts all boats"** When you invest in your own growth and that of your team, everyone benefits. As your team learns and develops new skills, they bring fresh ideas, solve problems more creatively, and drive innovation. It's a ripple effect that fuels sustained growth.

Building Systems That Scale

Another critical part of sustaining growth is making sure you have the right systems in place. When you're small or just starting out, you can get away with doing things manually or handling details personally. But as you grow, those systems need to evolve with you. What worked when you had a team of five won't work when you have a team of fifty.

Sustainable growth requires **scalability**. It's about putting processes in place that allow you to handle more without burning out. It's about automating where possible, delegating effectively, and ensuring that your systems can handle increased demand without sacrificing quality or efficiency.

Here's how you can build systems that scale:

- **Document Everything**: One of the simplest but most effective ways to prepare for growth is to document your processes. Whether it's how you onboard new team members, handle client interactions, or manage projects, having clear, documented procedures ensures consistency as you grow. And if someone leaves or transitions to a new role, you're not scrambling to figure out how they did their job.
- **Delegate Wisely**: We've talked about the importance of empowerment, and delegation is a big part of that. As your organization grows, you won't be able to oversee every detail, and that's a good thing. Empower your team by delegating responsibilities based on their strengths. Trust

them to own their areas, and focus your energy on the bigger picture.
- **Automate Where You Can**: Technology is your friend when it comes to scaling. Look for areas where automation can take tasks off your plate, whether it's project management, client communication, or internal processes. This frees up your team to focus on higher-value work and ensures that you're not bogged down by repetitive tasks as you grow.

People Are Still Your Greatest Asset

No matter how much you automate or how sophisticated your systems become, one thing remains true: **people are your greatest asset**. Without the right people, even the best systems will eventually crumble. That's why investing in your team is key to sustaining growth over the long haul.

- **Develop Future Leaders**: If you want your organization to continue thriving, you need to be thinking about leadership development. Who on your team has the potential to step into leadership roles? How can you mentor and develop them? Creating a pipeline of future leaders ensures that as your organization grows, you're not scrambling to find capable people to fill leadership positions. Start nurturing those leaders today.

- **Retention Matters**: Growth isn't sustainable if you're constantly losing your best people. Retaining top talent is essential to maintaining momentum. Make sure your team feels valued, recognized, and supported. Provide opportunities for advancement, offer competitive compensation, and create a work environment where people want to stay.
- **Foster Collaboration and Innovation**: Growth thrives in an environment of collaboration. Encourage your team to share ideas, solve problems together, and learn from one another. When you create a culture where people feel free to contribute and innovate, you're building a foundation for long-term success.

Service: Leading by Example

Sustained growth is anchored in the way leaders serve their teams. Leading by example means showing your team that you're willing to roll up your sleeves and support them in their work. It's demonstrating that leadership is not just about giving orders but being present, empathetic, and hands-on when needed.

Why is service so essential?

- **Builds Trust:** When your team sees you serving alongside them, they know you're invested in their success. This builds trust and loyalty, which are critical for sustained growth.
- **Strengthens Team Cohesion:** Service-oriented leadership fosters a culture where everyone feels they are part of something bigger. When leaders put the needs of the team first, it's easier for others to do the same, creating a unified and driven group.
- **Inspires Performance:** Leading by example motivates your team to put in their best effort. When they see you modeling dedication,

resilience, and adaptability, they're more likely to mirror those qualities in their own work.

Putting Service into Practice

1. **Be Visible and Engaged:** Don't just lead from behind a desk—be present. Walk the floor, check in with your team, and show genuine interest in their work. Engagement shows that you value their contributions.
2. **Listen and Act:** Being of service means listening to what your team needs and responding to those needs. Whether it's removing obstacles or providing resources, your actions speak louder than words.
3. **Show Empathy:** Understand that sustaining growth involves balancing productivity with well-being. Show empathy when your team faces challenges, and be there to support them through setbacks. Empathetic leadership creates resilience.

Adaptability: The Secret to Long-Term Growth

Let's face it—nothing stays the same forever. The strategies that got you to where you are today might not be the ones that will take you to the next level. That's why adaptability is so important when it comes to sustaining growth. The ability to pivot, evolve, and adjust your approach is what will keep you moving forward, even when the landscape changes.

Here's how you can build adaptability into your leadership and your organization:

- **Stay Curious**: Leaders who stay curious are always looking for new ways to improve. They ask questions like, "How can we do this better?" or "What's changing in our industry that we need to be aware of?" Curiosity leads to innovation, and innovation drives growth. Never settle for the status quo.
- **Be Willing to Pivot**: Sometimes the best-laid plans don't pan out, and that's okay. What's important is your ability to recognize when something isn't working and make adjustments. Whether it's changing your strategy, shifting

resources, or adopting new technology, being flexible and open to change is key to long-term growth.

- **Monitor Trends and Stay Ahead**: One of the best ways to stay adaptable is to keep an eye on trends in your industry or market. What's coming down the pipeline that could affect your organization? How are your competitors adapting? Staying informed allows you to anticipate changes and adjust before you're forced to react.

Mentorship: The Ripple Effect of Growing with Service

Service-oriented leadership doesn't just benefit your team—it impacts the entire organization. When leaders lead by example and prioritize service, it creates a ripple effect. Team members feel valued, trust is strengthened, and collaboration becomes more natural. This culture of mutual support and shared ownership is what sustains growth over the long term.

We talked earlier about the power of mentorship when it comes to self-awareness, but let's revisit it here in the context of **sustained growth**. Mentorship creates a ripple effect. When you mentor someone, you're not just helping them grow—you're helping the entire team grow.

Here's why mentorship is so critical to sustaining growth:

- **Passing Down Knowledge**: One of the biggest challenges of growth is making sure that institutional knowledge isn't lost. Mentorship allows you to pass down valuable insights, experience, and lessons to the next generation of leaders. This continuity is crucial as your organization expands.
- **Fostering a Growth Mindset**: Mentorship encourages a growth mindset in both the mentor and the mentee. When people see that growth and development are valued, they're more likely to push themselves to improve. As they grow, so does the organization. Again, it's that classic **rising tide lifts all boats** scenario—when one person succeeds, it positively impacts everyone.

- **Building Stronger Relationships**: Mentorship strengthens relationships within your team. It creates an environment where people feel supported, connected, and motivated to help each other succeed. This sense of community is essential for sustaining growth over time.

Resilience: Weathering the Storms

No matter how well you plan, challenges will come. Whether it's an economic downturn, a sudden shift in the market, or internal struggles, every organization faces setbacks. The question isn't **if** you'll face challenges—it's how you'll handle them when they come. That's where resilience comes in.

Building resilience into your organization is key to sustaining growth through tough times. Here's how you can do it:

- **Develop Problem-Solving Skills**: One of the best ways to build resilience is by creating a team of problem solvers. Empower your team to tackle challenges head-on. When people feel capable of addressing issues themselves, they become more resilient in the face of adversity.

- **Learn from Setbacks**: Failure is a part of growth. When setbacks happen, don't shy away from them. Instead, use them as learning opportunities. What went wrong? What can you do differently next time? Leaders who are willing to learn from failure come out stronger on the other side.

- **Build a Financial Cushion**: Growth can be exciting, but it's also risky. One of the best ways to sustain growth through tough times is by building a financial buffer. Make sure you're setting aside resources to weather unexpected challenges, so you're not caught off guard when things don't go as planned.

Key Takeaways

- **Sustained Growth Requires Service**: Leading by example and putting the team's needs first creates an environment where growth can thrive.

- **Adaptability and Continuous Learning**: Be open to change and encourage your team to learn and innovate. Growth and learning go hand in hand.
- **Empower Future Leaders**: Invest in developing your team to ensure growth continues beyond your leadership. People are your greatest asset—retain top talent and foster a collaborative, innovative culture.
- **Develop Scalable Systems**: Handle increased demand without losing efficiency or burning out your team by documenting processes, automating tasks, and delegating effectively.
- **The Ripple Effect**: Service-oriented leadership fosters a culture of trust and collaboration that sustains long-term growth.
- **Resilience is Key**: The foundation of sustained growth is resilience, allowing your organization to weather challenges and keep progressing.
- **Mentorship Creates Momentum**: Pass down knowledge, foster a growth mindset, and build strong relationships within your team to create a ripple effect of growth.

By leading with empathy, adaptability, and genuine support, you create a team that's not just successful but resilient, motivated, and ready for whatever challenges come their way.

Conclusion

Sustaining growth is more than maintaining momentum—it's about embedding service into your leadership and creating a foundation that can support success over the long haul. By investing in your people, building scalable systems, leading with empathy, adaptability, and genuine support, you create a team that's not just successful but resilient, motivated, and ready for whatever challenges come their way. You can ensure that your growth isn't just a spike, but a steady climb. And when you combine that with the power of service, mentorship, and resilience, you'll create an organization that not only grows but thrives, no matter what challenges come your way.

Remember, growth isn't the goal—**sustained growth** is. And with the right strategies in place, you can lead your team to success that lasts.

"You're off to Great Places! Today is your day! Your mountain is waiting, So... get on your way!" — *Dr. Seuss, Oh, the Places You'll Go!*

Conclusion:

Putting the K.E.Y.S. Framework into Action

You've now journeyed through the four essential parts of the **K.E.Y.S. framework**: **Know Yourself, Empower Others, Yield Results,** and **Sustain Growth through Service**. Each chapter has provided insights and practical strategies to help you lead with intention, purpose, and impact. But knowledge alone isn't enough — it's time to shift gears from understanding these principles to putting them into action. Because at the end of the day, leadership is more than just theory—it's what you do with that knowledge that counts.

It's easy to think of leadership as something abstract, full of big ideas and lofty goals. Leadership is practical. Leadership isn't a static skill. It's dynamic, evolving as you apply what you learn, reflect on your experiences, and adjust your approach. It's about decisions. It's about action. It's about people! The K.E.Y.S. framework was designed with that in mind. It's not just a set of high-level concepts; it's a roadmap for how to lead in a way that is not only effective but also people-focused, results-driven, and sustainable.

The key to making all of this work isn't about being perfect—it's about being **intentional**. Leadership is a journey, and like any journey, it requires continuous learning, reflection, and, most importantly, **action**.

Integrating the K.E.Y.S. Framework into Your Daily Leadership

1. **Start with Knowing Yourself.** Self-awareness is the bedrock of effective leadership. It's not just about understanding your strengths and weaknesses; it's about recognizing how your actions and decisions impact those around you. Make time for self-reflection, seek feedback, and commit to personal growth. This ongoing practice will ground your leadership in authenticity and confidence. Remember, when you know yourself

well, you make better decisions, inspire trust, and lead with genuine purpose.

2. **Empower Others to Thrive.** True leadership isn't measured by how much you can accomplish alone, but by how you inspire and elevate your team. Empowerment means trusting your people to take ownership, encouraging them to voice their ideas, and supporting them as they grow. When you empower others, you build a culture of shared success and innovation. Your team becomes more engaged and motivated, contributing their best work because they feel valued and trusted. This shared empowerment fuels not just immediate successes but sets the stage for long-term progress.

3. **Yield Results by Creating Space.** While achieving results is vital, the path to those results is equally important. Yielding results means striking the right balance between pushing for high performance and allowing space for team members to contribute meaningfully. Create environments where your team feels heard, involved, and motivated. This approach not only leads to better outcomes but also builds trust and

engagement. Leaders who yield space effectively foster creativity and innovation, as team members feel safe to explore new ideas and take risks. The result? Sustainable achievements driven by collective effort.

4. **Sustain Growth Through Service.** The final key is about long-term impact. Growth that lasts comes from a place of service and adaptability. Lead by example, be present, and show your team that you're invested in their success. Prioritize continuous learning, encourage innovation, and empower future leaders who can carry the torch forward. Service-oriented leadership means putting the needs of your team first and creating a supportive environment where people can thrive. Remember, sustained growth is anchored in service-oriented leadership—when you put the needs of the team first, you create a ripple effect that fuels resilience, trust, and sustained success.

Bringing the Framework to Life: From Theory to Action

So, how do you take these principles and apply them in your day-to-day leadership? Let's look at some practical steps you can take to bring the K.E.Y.S. framework to life:

Step 1: Know Yourself (And Keep Knowing Yourself)

Knowing yourself is not a one-time exercise—it's something that evolves over time. As you grow as a leader, your understanding of yourself will deepen. But that only happens if you're intentional about it.

- **Self-Reflection as a Habit**: Set aside time regularly to reflect on your leadership. How did you handle challenges this week? What are your strengths? What could you improve? This doesn't have to be formal—maybe it's during a walk, a quiet moment with your morning coffee, or journaling at the end of the day. The goal is to keep checking in with yourself.
- **Create Space for Input**: During meetings or discussions, consciously yield space for your team's contributions. Ask questions like, "What do you think?" or "How would you approach this?"

This not only brings fresh perspectives but also shows your team that their voices matter.

- **Commit to Lifelong Learning**: Whether it's reading, attending workshops, or working with a mentor, make learning a priority. The more you grow, the more you have to offer as a leader. And remember, learning isn't just about picking up new skills—it's about understanding yourself on a deeper level.

Action Step: Identify one area of your leadership that you want to improve. Set a specific goal and create a plan to work on it over the next three months. This could be improving your communication, managing your time better, or developing your emotional intelligence.

Step 2: Empower Others (And Watch Them Soar)

Empowerment is one of the most powerful tools in your leadership toolkit. When you empower others, you're not just helping them succeed—you're amplifying the impact of your leadership across your entire team.

- **Delegate with Trust**: One of the easiest ways to empower your team is through delegation. But don't just delegate tasks—delegate responsibility and trust them to own the outcome. Give your team the autonomy to make decisions, solve problems, and take risks. And when they succeed, celebrate it.
- **Mentor and Coach**: Empowerment is more than just delegation—it's about helping others grow. Take time to mentor and coach your team. Ask them where they want to go in their career and help them get there. Sometimes the most empowering thing you can do is simply believe in someone before they believe in themselves.
- **Create Space for Growth**: Empowerment doesn't happen in a vacuum. Create an environment where people feel safe to take risks, make mistakes, and learn. Encourage creativity, experimentation, and innovation. And when mistakes happen (because they will), focus on learning, not blame.

Action Step: Pick one person on your team who you think has untapped potential. Identify a project or responsibility you can delegate to them that stretches their skills. Offer support, but give them the freedom to take ownership and grow.

Step 3: Yield Results (With Purpose and People in Mind)

Yes, results matter—but **how** you get those results matters just as much. You want to hit your targets, but you don't want to do it at the expense of your team's well-being. Results that come from a place of purpose and alignment are the ones that last.

- **Set Clear, Measurable Goals**: Be specific about what success looks like. Your team can't deliver results if they don't know what's expected. But don't just set the goal—explain the **why** behind it. Help your team understand how their work contributes to the bigger picture. This adds meaning to the metrics.

- **Balance Accountability with Support**: Accountability is key to achieving results, but it needs to come with support. If someone isn't hitting their goals, don't just say, "Do better." Ask, "What's getting in the way, and how can I help?" Shift the conversation from blame to problem-solving.
- **Create Space for Input**: During meetings or discussions, consciously yield space for your team's contributions. Ask questions like, "What do you think?" or "How would you approach this?" This not only brings fresh perspectives but also shows your team that their voices matter.
- **Celebrate Wins Along the Way**: Results-driven cultures don't just focus on the finish line. They celebrate progress along the way. When your team makes strides—no matter how small—acknowledge it. This builds momentum and keeps morale high.

Action Step: Take a look at your team's goals for the next quarter. Are they clear and measurable? Does everyone understand why those goals matter? If not, take the time to communicate the bigger picture and align your team around a shared purpose.

Step 4: Sustain Growth (By Investing in the Future)

Growth is exciting, but it's not enough to grow—you have to ensure that growth is sustainable. This means thinking long-term, building systems that scale, and investing in the people who will carry your organization forward.

- **Build Scalable Systems**: As your organization grows, you'll need to put processes in place that can handle increased demand without sacrificing quality. Start documenting your key processes, delegating responsibilities, and automating tasks where possible.
- **Invest in People**: Growth is only sustainable if your team is growing too. Make leadership development a priority. Who are the future leaders on your team? What are you doing to develop their skills and prepare them for greater responsibility?

- **Stay Adaptable**: The strategies that got you to this point might not be the ones that get you to the next level. Stay flexible and open to change. Monitor trends in your industry, embrace new ideas, and be willing to pivot when necessary.

Action Step: Identify one process or system in your organization that needs to scale. Start working on documenting and improving it so that it can handle future growth. This could be anything from onboarding new employees to managing client relationships.

The Ripple Effect: How the K.E.Y.S. Framework Benefits Everyone

When you integrate the K.E.Y.S. framework into your leadership, the impact extends beyond you. **Knowing Yourself** builds confidence and clarity, which inspires trust. **Empowering Others** fosters a team culture where people feel valued and motivated. **Yielding Results** ensures that your pursuit of success is inclusive, balanced, and people-focused. **Sustaining Growth Through Service** creates a resilient, adaptable organization that thrives through collaboration and shared purpose.

Leadership isn't about doing everything perfectly; it's about being intentional, adaptable, and consistent. It's about understanding that your influence grows not just through your achievements, but through the growth, empowerment, and success of those you lead. When you lead by example and serve your team, you model the behavior that inspires others to take ownership and contribute to a collective vision.

Here's the most powerful part about putting the K.E.Y.S. framework into action: when you lead this way, everyone benefits.

- **Your Team** feels empowered, trusted, and valued. They know their work matters, they're growing in their roles, and they're invested in the success of the organization.
- **You**, as a leader, can focus on higher-level strategy because you're not bogged down by micromanaging. You have a team that can run with tasks, solve problems, and deliver results. You're leading, not just managing.

- **The Organization** thrives because it's built on a foundation of trust, accountability, and sustainable growth. You're not just achieving results—you're creating a culture where results are the natural byproduct of people who are motivated, aligned, and supported.

The impact of this approach is powerful. Teams that feel empowered and supported are more likely to innovate, tackle challenges head-on, and stay committed to shared goals. By leading with the K.E.Y.S. framework, you create a culture that thrives on trust, accountability, and continuous improvement.

Your Leadership Journey Continues

Leadership is a journey, and you now have the keys to navigate it with purpose. Take these principles and start incorporating them into your daily practice. Reflect on your progress, celebrate the small wins, and remain committed to growing both yourself and your team. Remember, the most impactful leaders are those who lead with heart, adapt with grace, and serve with dedication.

Look for opportunities to practice service-oriented leadership. Be the leader who shows up, supports, and listens. Empower your team by giving them room to grow and share their ideas. Focus on creating an environment where results are achieved through collaboration and shared effort.

You're equipped with the tools to make a lasting difference. Now it's your turn to unlock your full leadership potential and inspire those around you to do the same. The journey may not always be easy, but it will be rewarding, full of growth, and transformative for both you and your team.

The K.E.Y.S. framework is your guide, but it's **your actions** that make the difference. It's not about being perfect—it's about being intentional. Every day is an opportunity to lead with purpose, to empower others, and to make decisions that drive results and build sustainable growth.

You've got the tools. Now it's time to use them.

Final Thought

The best part about leadership? You're not in it alone. You've got a team, a purpose, and now, a framework to guide you. So, take the next step. Start with knowing yourself, empower your people, focus on yielding meaningful results, and commit to building something that lasts.

Your journey as a leader continues, and with the K.E.Y.S. framework, you're equipped to unlock your full potential—and the potential of those around you. Here's to the next chapter of your leadership story.

Lead with

K.E.Y.S.

and watch your leadership journey Transform.

-Patsy Alston

Additional Resources found at:

KLA.alstonent.com

YouTube @KeyLeaderA

KLA Mentoring Group

K.E.Y.S To 'People First' Leadership Workbook

90 day Leadership Journal with daily inspirations, insights, and reflection spaces

Weekly Planner with quotes to help you focus on you 'People First' Values

A 6 week course to help you adjust your mindset to connect to this leadership style

A 12 week mentorship program as an addition to the course to keep you on track and help you brainstorm solutions while you change your mindset.

A 1-day workshop explaining in detail the benefits of 'People First' leadership.

Motivational speaking engagements that will keep your leadership team going in the right direction.

Patsy Alston is a leadership expert, speaker, and co-founder of a coaching and consulting business dedicated to empowering leaders at all levels. In her over 20 years of experience in corporate and nonprofit leadership she developed the K.E.Y.S. framework: Know Yourself, Empower Others, Yield Results, and Sustain Growth through Service. When not coaching or speaking, she enjoys mentoring future leaders and creating systems that inspire growth and collaboration.

Patsy also co-leads a production company where she continues to drive innovation and collaboration and is a founding creator of KWĒN, an organization dedicated to empowering and inspiring women leaders by providing community, collaboration opportunities, and valuable resources and systems for building wealth.

www.ingramcontent.com/pod-product-compliance
Lightning Source LLC
Chambersburg PA
CBHW071653240526
45469CB00021B/2281